Living in Space

Contents

Where Do You Live in Space?

A space station is an **astronaut's** home in space. It is a space craft that stays in space and **orbits** the Earth.

The station provides everything astronauts need to stay alive. In space you cannot feel the force of **gravity** – everything floats about unless it is tied down. Everyday life goes on in space, but astronauts have to do some things a bit differently!

Astronauts float around the station because they are **weightless.**

The space station orbits high above the Earth.

What Do You Eat and Drink in Space?

Astronauts cannot cook in space, so they choose their food before they leave Earth. The food is cooked and packaged so that it does not go bad. The space station has an oven for warming up the food. Once the food is warm, each astronaut then attaches the packets they have chosen to a tray.

Each kind of food is put into separate packets.

Astronauts strap themselves to the walls of the space station while eating. This stops them from floating away.

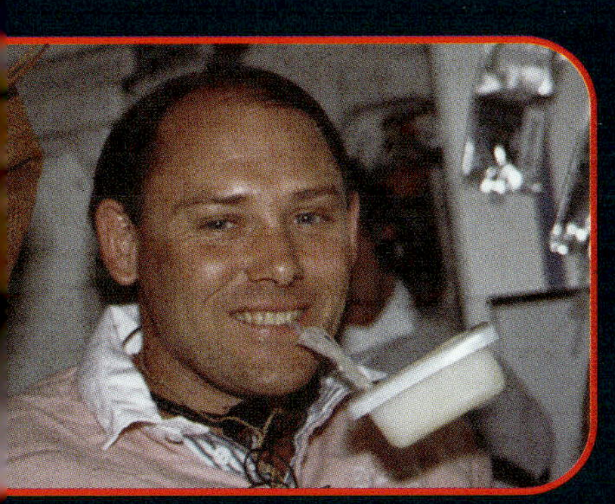

An astronaut drinks by sucking through a straw from a sealed can. The can is sealed to stop the liquid floating out of the can.

Sleeping

in Space

As the space station orbits the Earth, it changes from light to dark every hour and a half. Astronauts have to make their own night and day. They wear **eye masks** to block out the light so that they can sleep.

Astronauts sleep in sleeping bags. They strap themselves to the wall so that they do not float into anything while they are asleep!

The space station has tiny cabins with a sleeping bag in each cabin.

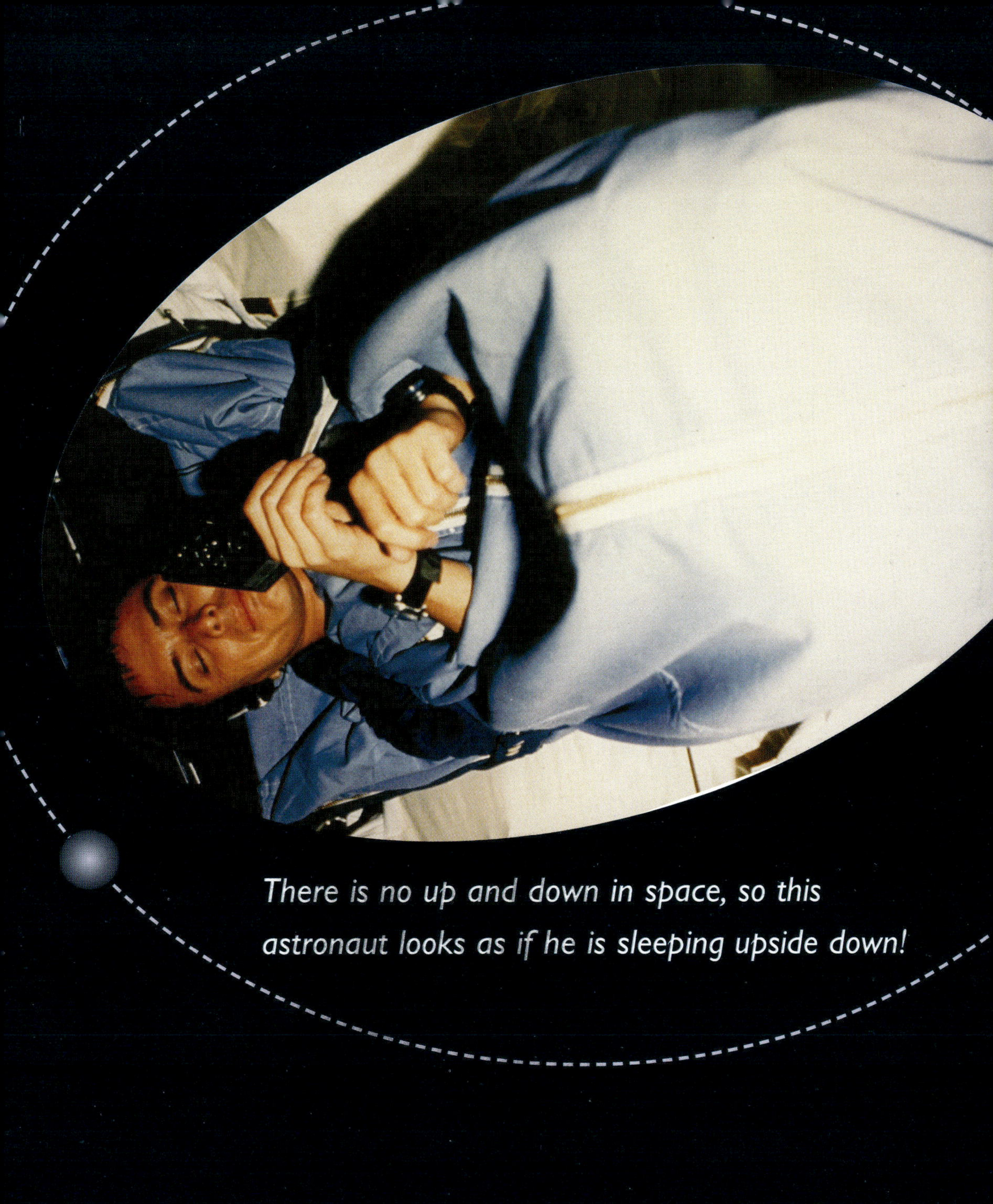

There is no up and down in space, so this astronaut looks as if he is sleeping upside down!

How Do You Wash in Space?

Water does not flow in space – it breaks up into tiny drops that float everywhere. Therefore, astronauts have special showers and toilets. The shower cubicle is **watertight**. The astronauts dry themselves by sucking up all the water from their bodies with a small vacuum.

Space toilets use air instead of water to suck away waste. The solid waste is dried and stored until it is taken back to Earth.

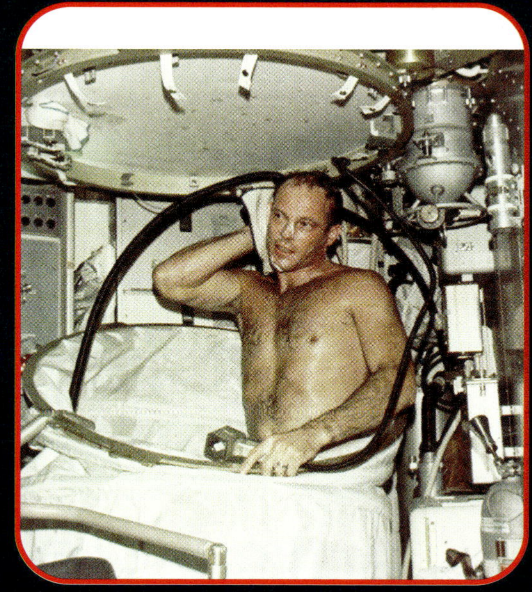

This astronaut is washing himself in a space station shower.

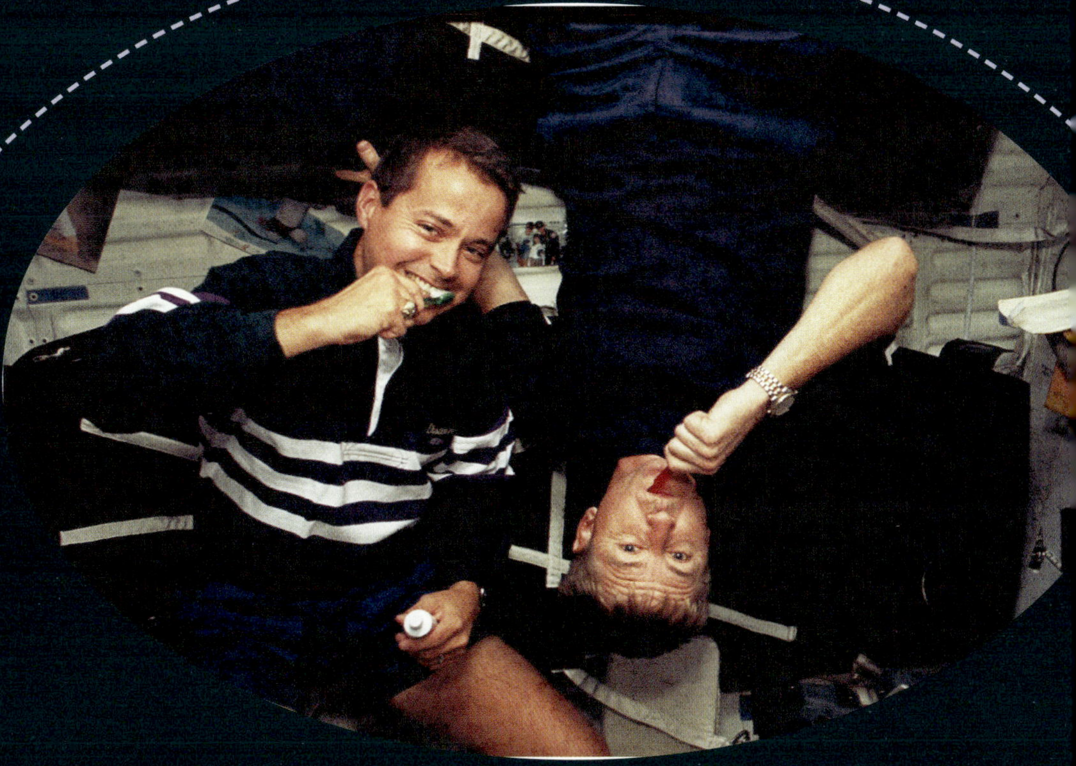

Astronauts can't spit in space, so they swallow their special toothpaste instead.

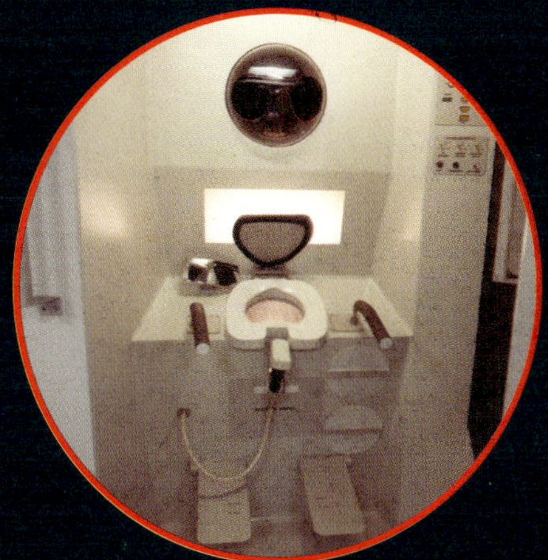

Hand bars and foot straps hold the astronaut onto the toilet.

in Space?

Floating in space is easy! It is so easy that astronauts have to use exercise machines to keep their **muscles** working. They are strapped to the machines so that they do not shoot off and float away. Astronauts exercise for at least two hours a day. If they don't their muscles become to weak that they cannot walk when they return to Earth.

Walking on a ***treadmill*** *helps to stop muscles becoming weak.*

Astronauts move around the station by pushing themselves off the walls.

How Do You Work
in Space?

Astronauts work hard in the space station. They do many experiments that help scientists on Earth. Some of the **experiments** prepare astronauts for longer space journeys in the future. For example, they study how their bodies cope with living in space.

Astronauts work outside the space station, too. They make repairs and they help to build new sections of the space station. They are often tied to the space station so they do not float away.

Experiments with plants will help future astronauts grow some of their own food.

Astronauts talk by radio to **Mission Control** every day.

The astronaut's **space suit** provides air and warmth. It has a **communication line** which allows the astronauts to speak to each other.

Having Fun
in Space

When astronauts have finished working, they relax and have fun. Each astronaut takes DVDs into space and sometimes all the astronauts watch films together. They even watch television when they can get a good picture. Sometimes astronauts just enjoy watching the stars or looking at the Earth far below.

Astronauts still enjoy hobbies such as reading and playing music in space.

Astronauts spend a long time together,
so it helps if they get on well.

Astronauts keep in touch
with their family and
friends by email.

Glossary

astronaut a person who travels into space

communication line a wire that carries voices, like a
   telephone wire

experiment a test to find out something

eye mask a strip of dark cloth that goes around your
   head and stops light getting into your eyes

gravity the force that pulls things towards the centre
   of the Earth

Mission Control people on Earth who are connected
   to the space station by computers and who help the
   astronauts in space

muscles the parts of the body that you use to move
   your bones

orbit to circle something

space suit special clothes that provide everything an
   astronaut needs when outside the space station in space

treadmill a machine that uses a moving belt so that you
   can walk or run without moving forward

watertight sealed so that water cannot get in

weightless not weighing anything on a weighing scale